To the second 1/3 of the Dads out there.

Please be patient. I promise to get to all of you.

Dad Joke Books from T. J. Alex:

Roll-A-Joke Books:

Roll-A-Joke Dad Jokes: Vol. 1
Roll-A-Joke Dad Jokes: Vol. 2
Roll-A-Joke Dad Jokes: Vol. 3
Roll-A-Joke Dad Jokes: Vol. 4
Roll-A-Joke Dad Jokes: Vol. 5
Roll-A-Joke Dad Jokes: Vol. 6

601 Dad Joke Books:

601 Dad Jokes; or Puns of the Patriarchy: Vol. 1
601 Dad Jokes; or Puns of the Patriarchy: Vol. 2
601 Dad Jokes; or Puns of the Patriarchy: Vol. 3

Dad Joke Coloring Books (Coming Soon):

Dad Jokes: The Coloring Book: Vol. 1
Dad Jokes: The Coloring Book: Vol. 2
Dad Jokes: The Coloring Book: Vol. 3

If you like this book, please leave positive feedback on Amazon!

601 DAD JOKES

Volume 2

WARNING

The most eye-rolling, groan-inducing, HEAD-SCRATCHING PUNS of ALL TIME!

T. J. Alex

XANDLAND XL PRESS

Published by Xandland Press

601 Dad Jokes: Volume 2 Copyright © T. J. Alex, 2025

ISBN-13: 978-1-95-492921-0

Printed in the United States

1 2 3 4 5 6 7 8 9 10 XP 30 29 28 27 26 25

If you shoot videos of your family enjoying this book and would like to be featured in social media, please email the footage to Xandland Press at info@xandland.com

To see what other Dad Joke books Xandland Press has to offer visit Xandland.com

About the Author:

T. J. Alex is the author of many Dad Joke books as well as a writer and editor on lots of other works. He also dabbles in screenplay writing.

He lives in Texas with his wife, three kids, and many, many, furry family members.

All of whom he tortures with the content you shall read here.

Introduction:

What makes the perfect Dad Joke? To me, it's two statements: a set-up and a payoff.

You'll see many joke books or social media pages that claim to tell Dad Jokes, but they will be full of questions with punch lines. For instance:

"Why did the scarecrow win an award? Because he was out standing in his field."

To me, that's not a Dad Joke. That's just a run-of-the-mill, ordinary joke. For it to be I Dad Joke, I'd rewrite it as:

"My scarecrow recently won an award.

He was out standing in his field."

See the difference? Two statements. Set-up. Payoff.

Probably 95% of the Dad Jokes in this book have been carefully chosen and re-written to make sure they not only meet my definition of a Dad Joke, but to also meet my high standards for humor and excellence.

Some people say I take this Dad Joke business too seriously, but I want the material I put out to be better than the rest.

Hopefully, you'll agree that this book, and the others I write, are outstanding in my field.

See what I did there?

My dentist told me that nitrous oxide is no laughing matter.

But I know that it is.

My wife told me that I scared her half to death when I came around the corner.

So, we're halfway there.

I'm never donating to anyone collecting money for a marathon again.

They just take the money and run.

The side of my beer can said, "Best drunk in January, 2025."

I'd like to thank the beer company for this prestigious award.

People always wondered why the Star Wars movies can out in 4, 5, 6, 1, 2, 3, 7, 8, 9 order.

Because in charge of scheduling, Yoda was.

After much consideration, Crackle and Pop have decided to retire.

It wasn't a Snap decision.

I got fired from work because I like to use my stress ball.

Apparently, you're not supposed to throw it at whoever stresses you out.

I had to tell my son he was adopted.

I was really hoping his new parents would be the ones to break it to him.

My boss at work told me to build two structures to hold water.

I said, "Well, dam!"

My wife is thinking of becoming a vegetarian.

I think that's a big missed steak.

When a genie granted me one wish, I told him I just wanted to be happy.

Now I'm living with six other dwarves and working in a mine.

I used to make a living changing light bulbs.

But I got burned out.

I think my wife is cheating on me. She told me, "I'll be home in ten...fifteen minutes max."

My name is not Max.

It's my first week working at the bicycle factory.

They already made me a spokes-person.

I asked Alexa what women want.

It hasn't shut up for 7 days.

I want to go on the record and say that I support farming.

You could call me protractor.

My girlfriend always comes home wearing a big hood, covered in bee stings, and smelling like honey.

I think I've got myself a keeper.

I have two tips on how to fall asleep in your recliner.

First, sit in your recliner. Second, be old.

You think you're bad at golf?

Join the club!

Three guys walked into a bar.

None of them ducked.

I asked my grandpa which walker he preferred.

He said Johnnie.

Next week is all about diarrhea awareness.

Runs until Friday.

When I was writing my autobiography, I accidentally spilled a bottle of glue.

That's my story, and I'm sticking to it.

My wife and I just celebrated ten years of a happy marriage.

Coincidentally, it was also our thirtieth anniversary.

I'm writing a book about voyeurism.

It's a peeping tome.

I asked my friend in North Korea what he think's of his country's leaders.

He said, "You gotta love 'em."

I renamed my toilet Jim instead of John.

Everyone is impressed that I go the Jim everyday.

A friend of mine asked me to invest in his line of new kitchen utensils.

But after reviewing the business plan, there were too many whisks.

My wife told me I needed snow boots.

Doesn't she know they would just melt?

My wife told me I was being immature.

So I kicked her out of my blanket fort.

My wife thinks we should regularly bathe our pigs.

Sounds like a bunch of hogwash to me.

My kids have told me I'm not allowed to tell dad jokes to their kids.

I guess I'll have to tell them grandpa jokes.

I was late for work because I stayed up so late cleaning.

I must have overswept.

⌣

My friend has asked me to give the toast at his sixth wedding.

I plan to open with, "Welcome back, everybody!"

⌣

My vet informed me he was going to have to put my St. Bernard down.

He was getting too heavy to carry.

⌣

I've chicken-proofed my lawn.

It's impeccable.

I can't believe I got fired from my job assembling clocks.

Especially after all the extra hours I put in.

The electrician and the stewardess are dating and it is going well.

Sparks are flying.

A friend of mine sued the airline who misplaced his luggage.

He lost his case.

Please be patient if you are trying to reach the Incessant Shouting Hotline.

They are currently experiencing high call volumes.

I made a ten-minute video of my shoes yesterday.

I got some really good footage.

If my wife and I are doing a cooking show.

It's really just a half hour of her telling me I'm in the way.

My dog always misinterprets things I say to him.

The other day I told him to heel. So he volunteered at the local hospital to do what he could.

I know a guy who toured Croatia.

He said it was fun, but the hotel was Hvar from satisfactory.

My doctor told me my prostate was perfect.

I was deeply touched.

Last night, knowing I had work in the morning, I slept like a baby.

I woke up crying every two hours.

I just found out Neil Diamond used to go by Neil Coal.

But then the pressure got to him.

I have a joke about a broken clock.

But it's not the right time.

My kids used to have a bedtime.

Now they just tuck me in and do whatever they want.

Good steak puns are hard to come by.

They're a rare medium well done.

I'd like to know how the earth rotates.

It would make my day.

I once knew a guy who had his entire left side cut off.

But he's all right now.

I refuse to help my son win a race against a dolphin.

That would defeat the porpoise.

My wife has threatened to leave me if I don't stop acting like a news anchor.

More on that when we come back.

My neighbor was absolutely sick when he got his high water bill.

I got him a get well soon card.

I asked the librarian where to find books on paranoia.

She leaned close and said, "They're right behind you."

My boss told me that as a security guard, I'm gonna have to watch the office.

I'm on season six, but I still have no idea what the show has to do with security guards.

Somebody asked me what to do with leftover bacon.

I'd never heard of such a thing.

My doctor told me I had the peek-a-boo virus.

He sent me straight to the I See you.

I never trust anyone who owns graphing paper.

They're always plotting something.

I think my wife is putting glue on my firearms.

She denies it, but I'm sticking to my guns.

My father is a bottle collector.

That sounds much better than alcoholic.

My New Year's resolution is to avoid anything that makes me look obese.

Pictures, mirrors, scales...

I've just had a stack of toilet paper rolls fall on me in the supermarket.

I'm ok, though. Just soft tissue damage.

On my ant farm, there's one ant that seems to have been shunned by the others.

He's a socially-dissed ant.

⌣

I saw the sword swallower from the circus buying some knives.

He must be on a diet.

⌣

The judge demanded I bring my pet skunk to the trial.

He wanted odor in the court.

⌣

I think my wife is starting to show the first signs of Alzheimers.

She said she can't remember what she ever saw in me.

My sister is always going on about photography jokes.

You can't shutter up.

I got fired from the calendar factory.

I guess I shouldn't have taken those days off.

The man calling the balls and strikes at my son's game is from Istanbul.

He's an Ottoman Umpire.

I just traded calamari for octopus.

It was a squid pro quo.

My dog is really smart. I asked my dog what is anything multiplied by zero.

He said nothing.

﹏

The fog has lifted.

It will be mist.

﹏

The police are looking for a man with one eye.

They'd find him faster if they used both eyes.

﹏

My friend just finished his sculpture of Jesus.

I think he nailed it.

I can't remember how to write 1, 1000, 51, 6, and 500 in Roman numerals.

I M LIVID.

No one has seen Santa since he GPS stopped working.

It's a lost Claus.

My wife told me to rub herbs on the meat for better flavor.

That's sage advice.

I quit my job as a bus driver.

I don't like people talking behind my back.

The psychic I went to was really overweight.

She was a four-chin teller.

I just wrote a book on reverse psychology.

Please don't buy it.

I've always thought the concept of trees to be suspicious.

They're all a bit shady to me.

Snow White must have been terrible to live with.

Six out of seven dwarves aren't happy.

I can tolerate algebra. Maybe a little calculus.

But graphing is where I draw the line.

I told my wife she drew her eyebrows too high.

She looked surprised.

I can't stop thinking of female superheroes.

I think I'm a heroine addict.

My son's rubber band pistol was confiscated by his algebra teacher.

It was a weapon of math disruption.

The female janitor at work asked me if I'd like go out with her sometime, but I turned her down.

I can't deal with high-maintenance women.

I'm going to get a pet termite and name him Clint.

Clint eats wood.

I always get heartburn when I eat birthday cake.

I'm going to start taking the candles off first.

Someone asked to buy my cow, but I don't think I can do it.

I've got too much steak in him.

My wife asks me to blow on her finger she'd burned on the stove.

But honestly, I'm not a fan.

3,025 years from now, life will either be really good or really bad.

It's 5050.

Tequila may not fix everything.

But it's worth a shot.

I was out hiking yesterday when I saw a cougar.

It almost made me puma pants.

I think I'm going to quit my job and clean mirrors for a living.

It's something I can see myself doing.

The shareholders of the compass manufacturer have fired the CEO.

There is concern the company isn't headed in the right direction.

The local smoke shop has been replaced with an apparel store.

Clothes, but no cigar.

My daughter told me she wanted an ice cream.

Unfortunately, my wife only gave us money for two beers.

I got fitted for a neckbrace years ago.

I haven't looked back since.

I suspect my wife is adding soil to my garden, but she denies it.

The plot thickens.

Someone accused me of impersonating a politician.

I was just sitting around doing nothing.

I know a lot of people named Will.

But most of them won't.

A shark can swim faster than me, but I can run faster than a shark.

In a triathlon, it would come down to who is the better cyclist.

Valley girls always gather in odd-numbered groups.

Because they can't even.

I dropped a can of paint on my boss on the job site.

Man, was his face red.

Eventually, Lizzie Borden made peace with her family.

They all buried the hatchet.

The other say I saw a fish swimming through the forest.

It must have been a tree sturgeon.

A girl I dated used to come over and clean my apartment.

She was maid for me.

My wife makes terrible coffee.

It's grounds for divorce.

The chimney sweep is the only one in town, and he knows it.

His prices are through the roof.

I'm writing a manual about hiking.

It's a step-by-step guide.

In the U.S. we call it an elevator, but in Europe, they call it a lift.

I guess we were just raised differently.

My wife was grateful that I helped make the bread.

But it was the yeast I could do.

A dentist once told me that brushing alone will not prevent tooth decay.

So now I have to find someone to brush my teeth with.

Two wrongs don't make a right.

But three lefts do.

I know this farmer who is too afraid to plant an orchard.

I told him he needed to grow a pear.

My wife gave me a to-do list, but I only did the first, third, and fifth things on the list.

She needs to understand that I only do odd jobs.

The police caught the criminal going down the stairs.

He was so con-descending.

Things were a lot tougher before the crowbar was invented.

Prior to that, crows had to drink at home.

Some people are pretty goood with PowerPoint.

But I Excel at it.

The janitor showed me his secret closet.

It was quite the supplies.

The guy who drives the ice cream truck is getting old.

He's been around the block a few times.

At my job interview, I filled my water glass until it overflowed a little.

I wanted them to see I always give 110%.

I only wear sleeveless shirts.

I have a right to bare arms.

I read an article about the dangers of drinking too much, and it scared me.

I'm never gonna read that again.

I used to like to flash people my booty.

But that was many moons ago.

A man died when a stack of books fell on him.

He only has his shelf to blame.

I want to see the movie Constipation.

But it hasn't come out yet.

Someone asked me why I got out of the elevator dressed so casually.

It's how I was brought up.

I know lots of jokes in sign language.

No one has ever heard them.

A lot of people are making jokes about the apocalypse.

They're telling them like there's no tomorrow.

My wife said she ran into a old friend at the supermarket today.

I guess she didn't see her standing there.

It's been six months since I joined the gym, and so far I'm not seeing results.

So tomorrow I'm going there in person to see what's going on.

My daughter has a chemistry test and asked me if I knew anything about sodium.

I said, "Na."

They told me I'd never be any good at poetry because I'm dyslexic.

But so far I've made three jugs and a vase and they're lovely.

A gang of dwarves tried to rob a butcher, but they didn't succeed.

The steaks were too high.

My friend wants to use a giant blender to power his speed boat.

But I think it's too big a whisk.

There are three kinds of people in this world.

Those that can count, and those that can't.

The funeral for the inventor of Tupperware has been delayed.

They can't find a lid to fit his coffin.

Bugs have diverse religious views.

They are all in sects.

Black holes and I are a lot alike.

I suck at everything, too.

We have a pretentious owl outside.

He says "whom" instead of "who."

I've heard Prague is a great place to vacation.

Think I'm going to Czech it out.

Highlighters are the pens of the future.

Mark my words.

I'm thinking of writing a book about fish puns.

So if you know any good ones, let minnow.

I'd like to get a new boomerang.

But I just can't seem to throw the old one away.

I parked in a bad neighborhood last night, and someone stole all my tires.

It was unwheel.

The local glassblower accidentally inhaled.

Now he's got a pane in his stomach.

My wife just stopped and said, "You weren't even listening, were you?"

That's a pretty weird way to start a conversation.

Bowling alleys are some of the quietest places.

In fact, you can hear a pin drop.

I'm extremely inspired by track runners.

They get over every hurdle in their way.

〰️

The waiter came to our table and said, "Sorry about the wait, sir."

Mentioning my weight problem was uncalled for.

〰️

My son asked me if I would tell him a potassium joke.

I said, "K."

〰️

I think the police are going to catch the bootlegger.

He can rum, but he can't hide.

I tried to be a ballet instructor.

But it was tu-tu difficult.

Scientists recently cloned a flea.

They made it from scratch.

My daughter lined up all her dolls in a perfect row.

It was a really good Barbie queue.

Most people think Mark Twain had a great sense of humor.

His son Choo Choo, not so much.

It used to be my dream to make the perfect bar of soap.

Somehow, that dream slipped away.

My doctor said, "I'm gonna be frank with you. You have cancer."

I said, "Can you not be Frank now? I'd like a second opinion."

Lawyers are always buried 12-feet underground.

Deep down, they're good people.

Some people confuse hippos and zippos.

But one of them is really heavy, while the other is a little lighter.

We always say that something is on fire.

In reality, it's the fire that's on something.

The ATM at the bank is addicted to money.

It's been having withdrawals.

I told my wife I had a crush on Beyonce, and she said, "Whatever floats your boat."

I guess she thought I said, "Buoyancy."

I just got diagnosed with Tom Jones syndrome.

It's not unusual.

My wife's female intuition is highly developed.

She knows I'm wrong before I even open my mouth.

My grandmother knew how to make the best ice cream.

Apparently, she went to sundae school.

My wife took my banana in the divorce.

I'm going to appeal.

Three conspiracy theorists walked into a bar.

You can't tell me that's a coincidence.

My wife is going to love the two banana peels I got her for her birthday.

She said she wanted a pair of slippers.

It'll be two more weeks before the scale I ordered online comes in the mail.

I can't weight.

I have no idea what HD is.

But my doctor said I had 80 of them.

My dog was chasing people on his bike.

I'm had to take his bike away.

I cut my finger shredding cheese.

I may have grater problems.

The best time on the clock is 6:30.

Hands down.

The police caught the guy who tickled another man to death.

I least I think that's what he did. The article said he was being charged with man's laughter.

My wife told me we would have less arguments if I wasn't so pedantic.

I told her that I think she means "fewer" arguments.

My son asked me who is the biggest rock group of all time.

I'm pretty sure it's Mount Rushmore.

My favorite teacher in school was Mrs. Turtle.

She tortoise well.

Koalas are my favorite animals.

They have many fine koalaties.

I stole my girlfriend's wheelchair when she left me.

And guess who came crawling back.

Everyone was astonished when the magician made his rabbit disappear.

But hare today, gone tomorrow.

Moses was quite the techie.

He was the first one with a tablet that downloaded data from the cloud.

My boss wanted me to email him a joke, but I emailed him back and said I'd have to do it later because I was busy.

He emailed me back and said, "That one's hilarious. Send me another."

I'm addicted to towels.

I can get dry any time I want.

I can't take my dog to the pond anymore because the ducks keep attacking him.

I guess that's what I get for buying a pure bread dog.

I just bought an Irish bread knife.

It's a four-loaf cleaver.

Is it crazy how saying sentences backwards...

Creates backwards sentences saying how crazy it is?

It's hard to take a good photo in a wheat field.

The image is always grainy.

My sister is always online looking for the perfect match.

I don't know why she doesn't use a lighter.

The local circus has hired a Filipino man to be their new contortionist.

He'll be their first Manila folder.

I asked my wife when her birthday is, and she said March 1st.

So I walked around the room and asked again.

I cut myself, but the cut didn't bleed.

I looked for blood, but it was all in vein.

Everyone laughed when the waitress asked if anyone knows CPR and I said I know CPR and 23 other letters of the alphabet.

Well, everyone except for that one guy.

I went to the aquarium this weekend, but I didn't stay long.

There's something fishy about that place.

I created a beer called Occasionally.

Now when asked, people can say, "I only drink Occasionally."

I went to the antique store and a friend I hadn't seen in years sold me a globe.

It's a small world.

I have a book coming out soon.

I don't know what possessed me to eat it in the first place.

I have a master's degree in being ignored.

But no one seems to care.

I would never survive if I had to hunt my own food.

I have no idea where tacos live in the wild.

My daughter asked me if the pool is safe for swimming.

Well, it deep ends.

The electricity company disconnected us last night.

We are powerless to do anything about it.

Diarrhea is hereditary.

It runs in your jeans.

I sued a man who shot me with a BB gun.

The case ended in a pellet court.

My deaf girlfriend told me that we needed to talk.

That was not a good sign.

I went to the library and the librarian had a sunburn.

She was well red.

I called Google Maps because my house doesn't show up on it.

But they refused to address it.

My wife asked me if I could fix dinner.

I had no idea it was broken.

My wife's underwear is too tight and revealing.

So she's making me get my own.

There's a new pill that cures procrastination.

I'm gonna take it someday.

I'm writing a book about bad weather.

It's only a draft at the moment.

Not one to brag, but I must really good with finances.

The bank calls me every day to tell me my account balance is outstanding!

At a celebrity event, I accidentally bumped into Dwayne Johnson's butt.

I hit Rock bottom.

I heard a kid was hit by a falling piano.

I bet he was A-flat minor.

I just saw a row of rabbits walking backwards.

It was a receding hareline.

My Fitbit watch congratulated me on a productive workout when my heartrate increased.

I was getting dressed.

I told my wife she looks better without her glasses.

She told me I look better without her glasses, too.

My wife said she has 14 reasons why she might leave me, including my obsession with tennis.

I said, "That's 15, love."

Once upon a time, King Arthur had too many knights at his Round Table.

He had a sir-plus.

Someone stole my anti-depressant pills.

I hope they're happy.

My wife told me that I needed to do something about the lights that keep going out.

I re-fused.

I recently opened a company selling trampolines disguised as prayer mats.

Prophets are going through the roof.

I couldn't tell if someone was waving at me or someone behind me.

It a related story, I lost my job as a lifeguard.

I'm thinking of taking up meditation.

It's better than sitting around and doing nothing.

My wife bought me a universal remote for my birthday.

This changes everything!

I saw a wicker furniture outlet in Copenhagen.

Something's rattan in the state of Denmark.

When I go to the gym, I usually hop on the treadmill.

But because everyone stared at me funny, I decided to run on it instead.

I grilled a chicken today.

But I couldn't force it to tell me which came first, or why it crossed the road.

I think I've got the coolest surgeon working on me.

People tell me he's a hip doctor.

I don't understand why some people choose to use fractions instead of decimals.

It's pointless!

If a cop ever pulls you over and says, "Papers?"

You should respond, "Scissors." That's how you beat a ticket.

My vacuum company went under, but I knew it was bound to happen.

All our products sucked.

This week will bring rane, hele, thundre, litnin, and frizzing colt.

It's a really bad whether spell.

The detective immediately identified the murder weapon.

It was a brief case.

I told my wife I wanted to be cremated.

She made me an appointment for Tuesday.

I got fired from the bank after a woman asked me to check her balance.

Apparently, I shouldn't have pushed her over.

I'm having trouble organizing a hide-and-seek league.

Good players are hard to find.

My friends think I'm addicted to brake fluid.

But I can stop whenever I want.

I left my job because I can't work for my boss after what he said.

He said I was fired.

My wife went to the doctor, and he told her that her DNA is backward.

AND?

I'm excited about the hot dog race on television today.

It's weiner takes all.

When I was locked out of my house, I got on one knee and talked to the lock in a calm, reassuring manner.

They say communication is the key.

Someone left some molding clay on my front porch.

I don't know what to make of it.

I passed all my classes except Greek Mythology.

It's always been my Achilles' elbow.

I want to find the doctor who messed up my limb-replacement surgery.

I'll kill him with my bear hands.

I was fired from my job at the park because I liked to arrange the animals by height.

They didn't like my critter sizing.

My brother and I aren't allowed to play with the chainsaw anymore.

Well...he's really my half-brother.

If you spell the words "Absolutely Nothing" backwards, you get "Gnihton Yletulosba."

Which means absolutely nothing.

Starting January 1st, I'm only watching movies in high definition.

It's my New Year's resolution.

I think my wife is upset because of how much money I spent on my new belt.

She says it's a huge waist.

The police asked me if I could identify the man who robbed the Apple store.

I was the only iWitness.

Last night I dreamed that my spirit rose from a toilet bowl.

It was an out of potty experience.

My copy of David Copperfield fell on my foot.

It hurt like the Dickens.

I had a fish that could break dance.

But only for about 20 seconds. And only once.

All chicken coops are only allowed to have two doors.

If they have four, they are chicken sedans.

My dog is going to college.

He's going to get his pedigree.

I love going outdoors.

It's much easier than going outwindows.

Things were heating up with my girlfriend, and she pointed to her bedroom and asked me if I had protection.

I said, "Why? What's in there?"

I thought I had a Japanese friend.

Turns out it was just my imagine asian.

At the new restaurant called Karma, there is no menu.

They just bring you what you deserve.

I hate it when people say age is just a number.

Age is clearly a word.

The Unabomber seemed to be angry with everything and everyone.

He had a short fuse.

There's a bee in our garage.

Now it's garbage.

My helium addiction is out of control.

But no one takes my cries for help seriously.

I have a joke about construction.

But I'm still working on it.

I dropped some corn flakes this morning and my wife stepped on them.

I had no idea I was living with a cereal killer.

My wife and I let astrology come between us.

It taurus apart.

Yesterday, I saw a mule with three legs.

It was a wonkey donkey.

I went to the boomerang store the other day.

They have a great return policy.

A man tried to sell me a coffin today.

That's the last thing I need.

I wish someone could tell me what IDK means.

Everytime I asked, they say, "I don't know."

Not to brag...

But I have enough money to live comfortably for the rest of the hour.

I used to work at a shoe recycling center.

It was sole-crushing.

A guy forgot his glasses and fell into a deep hole with water in it.

He couldn't see that well.

A policeman pulled me over and said, "I've been waiting all day for you."

I told him, "Well, I got here as fast as I could."

I'm a kleptomaniac. But if it gets too bad...

I'll take something for it.

Our town's plumber has been in business for 30 years.

He's become a regular fixture.

I put money into the coin machine over and over again.

But nothing ever changed.

My wife saw that my juice glass was empty and asked if I'd like another glass.

Why would I want two empty glasses?

My horse is going to be in a movie.

But it's only a bit part.

I've heard Cinderella was annoyed that her photos hadn't arrived.

But someday her prints will come.

My electrician takes karate classes to let off steam.

It's a much needed outlet.

My son's math teacher called him average.

I think he's mean.

Once I dated a girl from South Korea.

I really thought she was my Seoul mate.

My pet mouse "Elvis" died last night.

He was caught in a trap.

I remember when using Botox was taboo.

Now no one raises an eyebrow.

I'm going to try and attach a light to the ceiling.

I'll probably screw it up.

My friend thanked me when I bought him an elephant for his room.

I said, "Let's not talk about it."

I Just had a once in a lifetime experience.

I'll never do that again.

My son's tennis umpire was a little too agreeable.

He's generous to a fault.

I hate insect puns.

They bug the heck out of me.

I want to thank my legs.

They've always supported me. And my arms have always been by my side.

I keep asked people what LGBTQ stands for.

So far, I haven't gotten a straight answer.

My wife said she's leaving me because I act like I know everything.

I could have guessed as much.

Our local donut shop is closing after 30 years.

The owner says he's fed up with the hole business.

Our dentist is also a judge.

He pulls the tooth, the whole tooth, and nothing but the tooth.

When I bought a bunch of TV dinners at the store, the cashier said, "Wow, you must be single." I said, "You can tell just from the food I'm buying?"

She said, "No, it's because you're ugly."

My wife is not happy with her brain surgeon.

She gave him a piece of her mind.

My wife told me I should get in touch with my feminine side.

So I wrecked the car.

My dentist displays the award he won recently in his office.

It's a little plaque.

If a man speaks in the forest, and his wife is not there to hear him...

...is he still wrong?

My grandfather died when the doctor read his records and gave him Type-A blood.

Apparently, it was a Type-O.

William Shakespeare was a victim of cancel culture.

He was Bard for life.

My girlfriend texted me and asked if I'd like a toothpick, but I turned her down.

Just not that into pictures of teeth.

I thought Thursday was depressing, but then I waited two days.

That was a sadder day.

The hipster next door burned the roof of his mouth.

He ate his pizza before it was cool.

I had to evict my primary renters because of their drug use.

They were two high main tenants to me.

My wife threatened to leave me because of my obsession with optical illusions.

I said, "Wait! It's not what you think it is!"

A three-legged dog walked into a bar in the Old West.

He was looking for the man who shot his paw.

I got a flat tire while I was driving home the other day.

Must have been the fork in the road.

My doctor said I need to cut back on my sodium intake.

I took his advice with a grain of salt.

The waiter asked me how I found the steak.

It was easy. It was right next to the potatoes.

I'm going to an auction to bid on a house with a lengthy corridor, and I don't care how high the price goes.

I'm in it for the long hall.

I tried to change my network password to "hi-hat."

But apparently, the password cannot contain symbols.

I tell my wife all the time that I'm going to start jogging, and she just laughs.

It's a running joke.

My daughter started a business tying shoelaces on the playground.

It's a knot-for-profit.

The police finally found the nun who had been wandering all around town.

Apparently, she's a roamin' Catholic.

My wife thinks the birds aren't having fun in their cage.

But I suspect fowl play.

Instead of wearing glasses, I'm going to rub ketchup in my eyes.

They say Heinzsight is 20/20.

Someone asked me what I lion and a witch were doing in my wardrobe.

I told him it was Narnia business.

The police discovered the burglar after he fell into the cement mixer.

He's a hardened criminal.

My friend wants me to share the rabbit I killed when we were hunting.

But I'm not splitting hares.

***

While I was looking at different cars at the dealership, I said to the salesman, "Cargo space?"

He said, "Car no do that. Car go road."

***

I'd like to thank my student loans for helping me get through college.

I don't think I can ever repay them.

***

I'm hoping that my kids have all the things I could never afford.

Then I'm moving in with them.

The guy who has been stealing wheels off of cop cars hasn't been caught yet.

But they are working tirelessly to find him.

I once saw a koi wearing a bowtie.

It looked really sofishticated.

NASA is launching a satellite to say sorry to the aliens.

They're calling it the Apollo G.

I never buy anything with Velcro®.

It's a total ripoff.

My son asked me how one train can hear another train coming.

Obviously, with its engine-ears.

I saw an ad for a free TV, but the volume was stuck on high.

I couldn't turn that down.

I like to sleep with my clothes off.

Which is why my overnight commercial flight turned around and landed.

I lost my wife's audiobook last night.

Now I may never hear the end of it.

I just learned sign language.

It's pretty handy.

Hedgehogs are the stingiest of all animals.

They need to learn how to share the hedge.

I don't like to invite the optician to parties.

He always makes a spectacle.

I returned my new sweater because it held too much static.

They gave me another one free of charge.

I went to my bosses funeral, kneeled next to his coffin, and said...

"Who's thinking outside the box now, Walter?"

Let me know if someone has accused you of being born in a barn, and you'd like to talk about it.

My door is always open.

I haven't talked to my wife in five years.

I don't want to interrupt her.

I'll never pick a fight with an octopus.

It's always well-armed.

I don't have a black belt in karate.

I did get a black eye in karate, though.

My grandmother put wheels on her rocking chair.

I had no idea she was into rock and roll.

To the person who stole my place in line.

I'm after you now.

I've just finished reading The History of Soup.

It was the condensed version.

My neighbor came over at 2 a.m. to tell me he couldn't sleep.

Must have been his lucky day, because I was having a party at the time.

I wasn't sure how comfortable my new couch would be.

But sofa, so good.

I was kicked off the tug-of-war team.

They said I wasn't pulling my weight.

I have a new theory on inertia.

But it doesn't seem to be gaining momentum.

I'm thinking of taking up coin collecting.

I think the change will do me good.

I heard the police arrested the Energizer® Bunny™.

They charged him with battery.

I've stopped eating venison and switched to roasted pheasant.

Absolute game changer!

Later today, I'm gonna tell my son a joke about electricity.

He's gonna laugh until it hertz.

I didn't take the job because it's easy.

I took the job because I thought it would be easy.

NASA recently hired a claustrophobic astronaut.

He just needs some space.

I was fired from the keyboard factory yesterday.

I wasn't putting in enough shifts.

I don't pay attention to the annual silk worm race anymore.

It always ends up in a tie.

I started a business building yachts in my attic.

Sails are going through the roof!

I was happy about the belt I made out of groceries.

But my wife said it was a huge waist of food.

It's a little-known fact that Stalin only wrote in lowercase.

I read somewhere that he hated capitalism.

I got an email telling me how to read maps backwards.

It was spam.

It's Friday, and I have strep throat.

By tomorrow, I'm liable to have Saturday Night Fever.

The average height of an elf is three feet.

It's a little gnome fact.

I took my dog to the vet after he at all the scrabble tiles.

No word yet.

My wife wants me to stop telling breakfast puns.

But my son keeps egging me on.

Last night my wife and I watched two movies back to back.

Luckily, I was the one facing the TV.

Last night I went to a restaurant called Karma.

They serve just desserts.

My wife told me she wanted me to get a haircut.

But since she didn't say which one, I'm just going to get them all cut.

The man who runs the local bank quit his job.

He lost interest in everything.

I once worked as an ice delivery driver.

Coolest job I've ever had.

I married my wife for her looks.

But not the ones she's giving me lately.

So many people these days are too judgmental.

I can tell just by looking at them.

The wife asked me if I was drunk.

I feel like that's a loaded question.

I named my dog Five Miles.

Everyone is so impressed that I walk Five Miles every day.

This morning I found my son sleeping in the fireplace.

Apparently, he slept like a log.

Exercise helps with decision making.

I went for a jog this morning and decided to never do that again.

Police found an abandoned car with a set of gold clubs in the back seat.

They're still looking for the driver.

I know a woman who only dates men who own ladders.

She's looking for love in all the rung places.

My friend is a Buddhist, and refused Novocain at the dentist.

He wanted to transcend dental medication.

Yesterday I opened my water bill and my electric bill at the same time.

I was shocked.

I told the carpeters to carpet my floor, but not the steps.

They just gave me blank stairs.

I called 911 because my friend was bitten by a wolf. The operator asked, "Where?"

I said, "No, I'm pretty sure it was just a regular wolf."

I had a good joke, but there was a spelling error.

Now the whole joke is urined.

The pupils are the last part of the body to stop functioning when we pass away.

They die-late.

They found the remains of the ship on the ocean floor, and it was twitching.

It was a nervous wreck.

There's a company in town that makes yardsticks.

They won't be making them any longer.

Some guy asked me where he can get chicken stock in bulk.

But I told him to try the stock market.

Someone told me how to make my own holy water.

They said to just boil the hell out of it.

At the job interview, I was told I'd start out at $35,000, but later I can make around $50,000.

So I told the interviewer I would come back later.

I just blew some of the powered sugar off my donut.

Dieting is hard.

My wife dropped the laundry basket. It was terrible.

All I could do was stand there and watch it all unfold.

I told my wife that for twenty-six years, all she's ever done is point out my mistakes.

She said, "Twenty-seven years, honey."

I started getting up on the left side of the bed in the mornings.

But it just doesn't feel right.

I know a comic-book illustrator who is completely biased.

He's always drawing his own conclusions.

My wife said she had blisters on her hand from the broom.

I told her to take the car next time.

I'm sick of people saying the United States it he stupidest country in the world.

I think Europe is the stupidest country.

My wife told me that for Christmas, nothing would make her happier than a diamond necklace.

So I bought her nothing.

I'm terrified of elevators.

But I'm taking steps to avoid them.

I have a joke about communism.

But it's only funny if everyone gets it.

My wife asked me to put ketchup on the shopping list.

Now I can't read the shopping list.

My friend applied to be a mailman, and I told him to let me know how it goes.

He said he'd keep me posted.

Dr. Franenstein went to a bodybuilding competition.

It was a terrible misunderstanding.

I keep telling my dad to get a new hearing aid.

But he just won't listen.

A doctor broke his leg while auditioning for the play.

Luckily, he made the cast.

When I eat Italian, I always asked for a box to take home my leftovers.

A penne saved is a penne earned.

The dry cleaner was indicted for money laundering.

But a deal is being ironed out.

I have a great relationship with my furniture.

Me and my recliner go way back.

Last night I saw a burglar kicking in his own door.

He must have been working from home.

My daughter finally overcame her fear of snakes.

Addergirl!

I frequently like to buy pants, and then have then taken out.

I do it all the time: buy, enlarge.

I'm not sure I believe all this stuff about genetically-modified food being bad for you.

I just had a really tasty leg of salmon, and I feel fine.

Someone broke into my house last night looking for money.

I told him to let me know if he finds any.

My wife said she's making me a reversible jacket for my birthday.

I can't wait to see how it turns out.

Everywhere I go, it feels like a wading bird is following me.

I think I'm being storked.

My wife is a nurse, so I always give her red markers for Christmas.

In case she has to draw blood.

"I am" is the shortest sentence in the English language.

But "I do" is the longest sentence.

My friend bought me a telekinetic abacus for my birthday.

I wasn't my favorite gift, but it's the thought that counts.

I can finally admit that I shouldn't have eaten all those lions.

It took me a long time to swallow my pride.

A friend of mine visited Stockholm, but was having trouble sleeping.

I wished him Swede dreams.

I recently visited conjunctivitis.com.

Now that's a site for sore eyes!

My wife and I had a really good relationship until we bought a waterbed a few months ago.

Now we've just sort of drifted apart.

I'm a very competitive person.

And I'll be the first to admit it.

People were dismayed that I didn't know what the apocalypse means.

But it's not like it's the end of the world.

I have a bad feeling about my calendar.

It's days are numbered.

A truck carrying strawberries turned over on the Interstate.

It caused quite the traffic jam.

My friend jumped out from around the corner and scared the crap out of me.

With friends like that, who needs enemas?

I suffer from CDO.

It's like OCD, but more conveniently put in alphabetical order.

I was fishing, and someone yelled at me from across the river and asked me how to get to the other side.

He must not have been very bright. He was already on the other side.

When I worked as a butcher, a lady asked me if our turkeys got any bigger.

She's not too smart. How can dead turkeys get bigger?

I start every phone conversation with, "My phone is almost dead."

That way I can hang up whenever I want.

I just found out my father was a mime.

He's kept that quiet for a long time.

My wife asked me how many paranoid people it takes to screw in a light bulb.

I asked her, "Who wants to know?"

I'm working on a joke about beds.

But I haven't finished making it up yet.

Purple is my favorite color.

I like it better than blue and red combined.

I think it's possible my Dad jokes are too cheesy...

Everyone seems to be laugh-tose intolerant.

I heard a woodworker went to the bank.

He wanted to open a shavings account.

My wife says she will not spread my remains in the river when I die.

It has something to do with my refusal to be cremated.

My son took a fork to his math exam.

His teacher had told him it would be a piece of cake.

I decided to get a brain transplant.

Then I changed my mind.

Chances are, if you've seen one shopping center...

...you've seen the mall.

The employee labor shortage is getting really bad.

Now even long-haired freaky people can apply.

I used to be addicted to swimming.

But I've been dry for six years.

A farmer plowed his field with a steamroller.

He wanted to grow mashed potatoes.

I read an article that said cigarettes can harm your children.

Which is why I now put my cigarettes out in the ashtray now.

I think my email system has been corrupted.

The Outlook doesn't look good.

I saw that trampolines are half off today.

I jumped at the offer.

I knew the spray paint company was going to go out of business.

I could see the writing on the wall.

Someone stole my sleeping mask.

I won't rest until I find out who.

I was on a diabetes-awareness site, and it asked me if I would accept cookies.

Duh. Why do you think I'm on your site?

If two vegans get in an argument...

no one can call it a beef.

I like to take my cow on a walk through the local vineyard.

I herd it through the grapevine.

I hear there's a new type of broom out.

Apparently, it's sweeping the nation.

I told my wife I'm going to burn 2,000 calories today.

So I'm leaving the pizza in the oven too long.

I had a nightmare that disco music was making a comeback.

At first, I was afraid. I was petrified.

It cost a lot of money when I dropped the cable box on my foot.

I had to see a doctor out of network.

My brother bought me a mind-controlled calculator.

It's the thought that counts.

I like to tell jokes to my cows.

They're a laughing stock.

I fell in love with a girl who ended up becoming a nun.

She was a hard habit to break.

Guess who I ran into one the way to the eye doctor.

Everyone.

A wizard asked me to proofread one of his scrolls last week.

Actually, it was more of a spell check.

The most crucial part of any joke so that people—

Timing!

My dad was born a conjoined twin, but they were separated at birth.

I have an uncle, once removed.

I've heard people in Afghanistan aren't allowed to watch television.

My wife recently told me I had a smokin' hot body.

Well, those weren't her exact words, and my clothes were on fire at the time, but I think that was the jist of it.

I've heard people in Afghanistan aren't allowed to watch television.

Apparently, there's a telly ban.

I got home and discovered my kids were still on Ebay.

If they are there tomorrow, I'll lower the price.

My doctor said to get in shape, I need to start doing lunges.

That would be a big step forward.

My sister bought me a dictionary that isn't in alphabetical order.

I can't find the words to thank her.

Once I competed in the lazy Olympics.

I came in 4th just so I wouldn't have to walk up to the podium.

The jury didn't prosecute the man who stole the gate.

They were afraid he'd take a fence.

I saw a guy yesterday with a wheel barrow full of four-leaf clovers.

He was really pushing his luck.

Scientists are studying how alcohol effects how drunk people walk.

So far, the results are staggering.

My wife isn't talking to me because I tell too many bird puns.

Well, toucan play at that game.

I woke up in the emergency room only to be told I'd been hit by a stampede of wildebeests.

The gnus hit me hard.

I didn't think my sister would like Cuba.

But it turns out she's Havana good time.

I think the invention of the wheel was the most important invention in human history.

It's what got things rolling.

I have a friend who is a sharpie addict.

He's always blacking out.

I entered a barber contest, but got disqualified.

They found out I took a short cut.

My daughter's not getting anywhere in her geometry class.

It's like she's going in circles.

I did a theatrical performance about puns.

It was a play on words.

Meteorologists recently weighed rainbows.

They're pretty light.

I tried to walk like an Egyptian.

Now I need to see a Cairo-practor.

I heard that the guy who invented Velcro died.

RIP.

My brother bought me a mind-controlled calculator.

It's the thought that counts.

My ex-wife misses me.

But her aim is improving.

My wife threatened to leave me because she says I have filthy and disgusting habits.

I was so shocked, I nearly choked on my toenails.

My kids refused to eat leftover tacos, so my wife said to throw them out.

But now what am I supposed to do with all these tacos.

The funeral director tried to fly two bodies across the country.

But the airline only allowed one carrion per passenger.

When I was a hipster, I would do something before it was cool.

Which was great until I tried ice skating. I nearly drowned.

My boss told me to have a good day.

So I went home.

I went to the zoo yesterday and saw a baguette in a cage.

Apparently, it was bread in captivity.

Is it okay that I use barbed wire to strain my food?

Or is that a fence sieve?

I know a bald man who keeps a comb in his pocket.

He just can't part with it.

Our pig seems to have lost its voice.

It has become disgruntled.

I can't decide if I want to be a hairdresser or a story writer.

It's a toss-up. Heads or tales.

The local auctioneer died yesterday, and he was really young.

20? 25? Did I hear 30?

A man was admitted to the hospital because he tried to eat a horse.

His condition is stable.

I've joined a self-help group for people who talk to much.

It's call On-and-On Anon.

Justice is a dish best served cold.

If it were served warm, it would be justwater.

Most graveyards are overcrowded.

People are always dying to get in.

An old high school buddy looked me up after he drank an invisibility potion.

Long time, no see.

The branch of the local satanic cult just kicked me out!

And after all the sacrifices I've made!

My new thesaurus is terrible.

In fact, I'd say it's terrible.

My wife wants our water bed to be bouncier.

So I'm going to add some spring water.

When my wife was in labor, I told her jokes to distract her from the pain, but she didn't laugh.

Must have been the delivery.

There aren't a lot of people going into botany these days.

You'd think it'd be more poplar.

The older I get, the more I think about all the people I've lost over the years.

Perhaps a tour guide wasn't the best career choice.

I used to have an irrational fear of speed bumps.

But I slowly got over it.

All the waterfowl kept their eyes closed except for one.

It was a Peking duck.

I knew I magician who lost his magic.

Now he's just ian.

A boiled egg makes a great breakfast food.

It's hard to beat.

I told someone that I love my job as an Uber driver because I'm my own boss and no one tells me what to do.

He said, "Turn left here."

My daughter couldn't wait to meet my sister.

The aunticipation was killing her.

Today my son asked, "Can I have a bookmark?" And I bursts into tears.

Eleven years old, and he won't call me dad. And my name's not even Mark!

Do you think I second-guess everything I do?

Or is it just me?

My daughter bought me an alarm clock that calls me names to wake me up.

That was a rude awakening.

People say that talk is cheap.

Those people have clearly never spoken to a lawyer.

I gave my wife a dart and told her to throw it at the map to determine where we're going on vacation.

Looks like we're spending a week behind the fridge.

My wife won't let me eat dessert.

I'm not pudding up with it.

My house is haunted by a chicken.

It's a poultrygeist. I'm calling an eggsorcist.

There's a word I always spell incorrectly.

It's incorrectly.

My friend David lost his ID.

Now he's just Dav.

I don't trust acupuncturists.

They're all a bunch of backstabbers!

The beekeeper was arrested after he confessed to stealing from his job.

They've charged him with em-bee-zlement.

The nude bathers got angry when the police told them to put some clothes on.

They didn't care for their Coppertone.

Puns never work on kleptomaniacs.

They take everything literally.

I can't believe I forgot to go to the gym today.

That's five years in a row now.

I spent a lot of time and money childproofing my home.

But the kids still manage to get in.

My son asked me why cowboys like to ride horses.

Well, obviously, they're too heavy to carry.

I have a friend who has started drinking wet cement.

He's going to get stoned.

I wanted to buy twelve bees from the beekeeper, but he insisted I take thirteen.

It was a freebee.

⚬⚬⚬

Once I bought a thesaurus and all the pages were blank.

I have no words to describe how angry I was.

⚬⚬⚬

A number in the bathroom stall promised a good time if I called it. So I did.

The girl who answered showed me she could run a 40-yard dash in five seconds flat.

⚬⚬⚬

I went to the psychic and accidentally broke her crystal ball.

It cost me a fortune.

I've come to terms with the fact I'll never get down to my original weight, and I'm okay with that.

After all, 7 lbs. 2 oz. is just not realistic.

My wife has been missing for a week, and the police told me to prepare for the worst.

So I went to the thrift store and got all her stuff back.

In every marriage, one person is always right.

The other person is the husband.

My son asked me how many apples grow on our apple tree.

Well, obviously, all of them.

The waiter asked, "Comfortable, sir?"

I said, "No, come for food."

Argentina is surprisingly cold.

In fact, it's bordering on Chile.

I just visited the farm where Doritos are made.

It was a cool ranch.

Swords will never be obsolete.

They are cutting-edge.

My grandfather passed away at 101.

He died in his prime.

I'm proud of my son for becoming an organ donor.

It takes guts.

I usually dream in blue.

It's a pigment of my imagination.

I like waiters.

They bring a lot to the table.

A red ship and a blue ship collided at sea.

Last I heard, the survivors were marooned.

I recently went to the annual Plastic Surgery Addiction Conference.

It was great to see some old friends and lots of new faces.

My son told me I could write better if I'd let him sharpen my pencil.

He makes a good point.

My son asked me what it's like being a parent.

So I woke him up at 2 a.m. to tell him I had to pee.

I went to the wedding of two satellite installers.

The reception was fantastic.

Doctors told me to eat only dried, salted meats for a month.

I've been cured.

My wife told me she wants to double our money.

So I gave her a mirror.

A friend of mine has a cat with eight legs.

It's an octopuss.

A rancher I work for told me to round up his 97 cows.

So, now he has 100 cows.

My college degree was rolled up like a tube when they gave it to me.

It was a graduated cylinder.

I went to a haunted bed and breakfast in France.

That place gave me the crepes.

I asked the baker how he made his bread.

He said that information was on a knead-to-know basis.

I stepped on a grape today.

It let out a little wine.

A lot of people are jumping off the Paris bridge.

Those people are in Seine.

I don't trust stairs.

They're always up to something.

I bought a pair of tortilla chip swimming trunks yesterday.

Might go for a dip later.

My wife's old boyfriend refused to eat anything that had fruit in it.

She had to let that mango.

Someone came by the house today looking for donations for the community swimming pool.

So I gave him a glass of water.

On a flight, I got tired of arguing with a man who claimed I was in his seat.

I finally said, "Fine, you fly the plane!"

I used to believe my dad got fired as a road worker for theft.

When he got home, all the signs were there.

The best business to be in is selling stoves.

You'll always offer a range of hot products.

My wife and I argued over what was the ninth letter in the alphabet.

I was right.

I always carry a concealed knife.

Most people don't see the point.

I'm engineering a new pill that's 50% glue and 50% aspirin.

For people with splitting headaches, of course.

My copy editor wasn't able to correct my manuscript today.

She told me she was il (sic).

Farmers make the best D.J.s.

They know how to drop the freshest beets

I'd love to have kids one day.

Two days, tops.

My girlfriend and I are going together to get new glasses.

After that, we'll see.

People were waiting in line to play a giant Scrabble game at the park.

I wanted to play, but the Q was too big.

I only eat watermelon with seeds.

I support plant parenthood.

My tape measure, yard stick, and ruler were on the kitchen counter this morning.

I feel like something's a foot.

My son asked me the difference between ignorance and apathy.

I don't know, and I don't care.

I used to hate facial hair.

But it grew on me.

My friend confessed to eating a whole box of Kinder Eggs.

He's full of surprises.

A history degree is useless.

There's no future in it.

The school's band director asked if I could make a bandstand.

So I took away their chairs.

Once I misspelled a person's name on a headstone.

It was a grave mistake.

My wife said she was surprised by how little people change.

I would assume it's the same process, but their clothes are just smaller.

My wife asked if I wanted tuna fish.

I didn't know fish had one knee, much less two.

A really weird thing happens if you cut off your left arm.

Your right arm will be left.

You don't need a parachute to go skydiving.

But you do need a parachute if you want to go skydiving twice.

Even before I had kids, I liked to tell dad jokes.

Back then, I was a bit of a faux pa.

It snowed last night, and it looks like Will Smith was walking around my yard.

Those were some really fresh prints.

Once I thought I made a mistake.

But I was wrong.

I'd like to know where a guy can find a person to hang out with.

I'm asking for a friend.

The neighborhood barber was arrested for selling drugs.

I was a customer for six years. Who knew he was a barber, too?

There's one celebrity who is always ready to eat cereal.

It's Reese. With her spoon.

I once proposed to my Irish girlfriend with a fake diamond ring, and she refused.

She knew it was a sham rock.

I'm reading a book about lubricants.

It's non-friction.

My wife was mad after she told me to buy six Sprites on the way home.

Apparently, I picked 7 up.

I was going to propose to my girlfriend, but the dog ate the ring.

Now it's just a diamond in the ruff.

I can never take my son to the beach again.

In retrospect, naming him Shark my not have been a good idea.

I wrote a song about tortillas.

Actually, it's more of a wrap.

More from Xandland Press

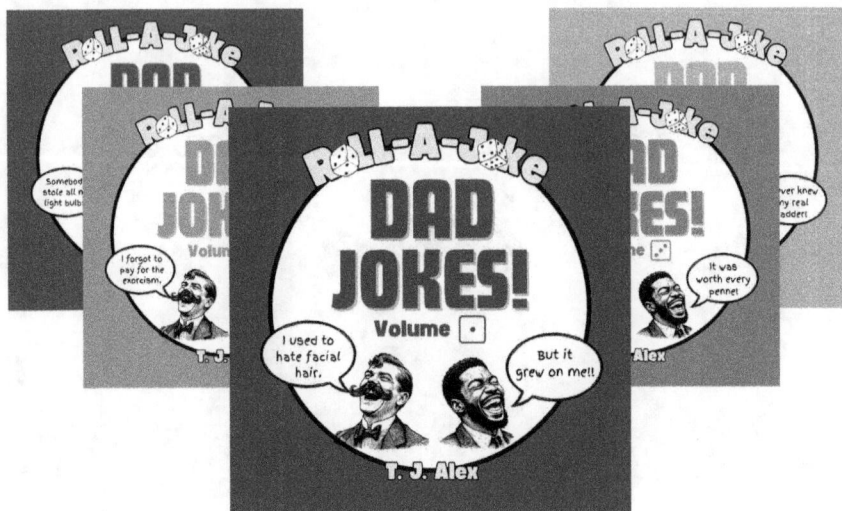

Roll-A-Joke Dad Joke books (6 Volumes):

Roll the dice to find out which Dad Joke
your kids will be subjected to!
Provides HOURS of fun and laughs (or groans)!

The Dead Fall series
by Joseph Xand:

Zombie novels that
have been compared
to Stephen King's
The Stand and
The Walking Dead.

Nosferatu:
A Symphony of Horror

A novelization of the classic
1922 film, written by Joseph
Xand and edited by T. J. Alex

www.ingramcontent.com/pod-product-compliance
Lightning Source LLC
LaVergne TN
LVHW051411080426
835508LV00022B/3039